# ADDRESS

ILLUSTRATIVE OF THE

# NATURE AND POWER OF THE SLAVE STATES,

AND THE

# DUTIES OF THE FREE STATES;

DELIVERED AT THE REQUEST

OF THE

INHABITANTS OF THE TOWN OF QUINCY, MASS.,

ON THURSDAY, JUNE 5, 1856.

---

BY JOSIAH QUINCY.

---

Altered and Enlarged since Delivery.

---

BOSTON:
TICKNOR AND FIELDS.
M.DCCC.LVI.

## Dedicated

TO

# THE PEOPLE OF THE FREE STATES,

WHO ARE ENTREATED TO CONSIDER THE VIEWS AND STATEMENTS IT PRESENTS.

---

THE question to be decided, at the ensuing Presidential election, is, Who shall henceforth rule this nation, — the Slave States, or the Free States? All the aspects of our political atmosphere indicate an approaching hurricane. Whether it shall sweep this Union from its foundations, or whether it shall be prosperously weathered, depends, under Heaven, on the man whom the people shall choose to pilot them through the coming storm. In my judgment, that man is JOHN CHARLES FREMONT. I have not, and never had, any connection with the party that selected him. Personally, I know him not; but I have read the history of his life, and believe him to be a man as much marked out by Providence for the present exigency of our nation as Washington was for that of our American Revolution.

He comes, from whence great men usually do come, from the mass of the people. Nursed in difficulties, practised in surmounting them; wise in council; full of resource; self-possessed in danger; fearless and foremost in every useful enterprise; unexceptionable in morals; with an intellect elevated by nature, and cultivated in laborious fields of duty, — I trust he is destined to save this Union from dissolution; to restore the Constitution to its original purity; and to relieve that instrument, which Washington designed for the preservation and enlargement of freedom, from being any longer perverted to the multiplication of Slave States and the extension of slavery.

JOSIAH QUINCY.

QUINCY, July, 1856.

# ADDRESS.

Fellow-Townsmen, — I come, at your request, in the spirit of liberty and truth, to speak on topics worthy to be heard and pondered by you and every inhabitant of the Free States of this Union. They will relate to your liberties and duties. The former has been struck down in the Senate Chamber, at Washington, by slaveholders. In Kansas, the blood of freemen has been shed, by the pistols and bowie-knives of slaveholders, under circumstances of unparalleled violence. What place more suitable to speak words of boldness concerning the obligations of freemen, or with more hope of effect, than in the north precinct of the old town of Braintree, now Quincy, where those devoted assertors of liberty, John Adams, John Hancock, Josiah Quincy, jun., and John Quincy Adams, were educated, and passed their youth, and where the graves of three of them are within the hearing of my voice?

In early life, from 1805 to 1813, I served as Representative in the Congress of the United States from the town of Boston. I was an active member of the Federal party formed by Washington, and have never belonged to any other. Though sympathizing in feeling with Free Soilers and Abolitionists, I have never concurred in the measures of either. My heart has been always much more affected by the slavery to which the Free States have been subjected, than with that of the negro. Placed successively, since 1820, in the offices of Judge of the Municipal Court, of Mayor of Boston, and of President of Harvard College, I have abstained from all connection with politics for *thirty-four years*, except by voting; and now I come, at your request, to offer views and opinions on the present crisis of public affairs, derived from the light of history, and from the counsels and advice of Washington.

The blow on the head of Sumner was not intended for him alone. It was struck at Liberty herself, in one of her most sacred temples. It was a public notice and declaration, to every man in the Free States, that liberty of speech no longer existed in Congress for him or for his Representative; that whoever, coming from the Free States, dare to utter a word in opposition to the views, or in derogation of the power, of slaveholders, will speak at the peril of life. There is nothing new in this system of intimidation. Fifty years ago, it was an approved practice of slaveholders. In that day, men from the Free States, who were open opponents to the administration, often carried pistols in self-defence. Others, urged by their friends to do it, declined; being unwilling, under any circumstances, to have the life of a fellow-being on their consciences. The only difference between our times and the past is this: heretofore they brandished the bludgeon; now they have brought it down. Formerly the bowie-knife was only seen in its sheath, or half-drawn by way of terror; now it is seen glistening in their hands, or steeped in the blood of freemen in Kansas.

This state of things naturally leads thoughtful minds to reflect on the actual condition of this Union, — of Slave States politically united with Free States. Those living under the former are in a perpetual consciousness of danger.

It cannot be otherwise, however they may attempt to conceal it from others and from themselves. It is impossible that *three hundred thousand whites*, who are the masters, surrounded by *three million of blacks*, who are slaves, can live otherwise than under a never-ceasing sense of danger. The mode of maintaining the subjection of their slaves is, therefore, the constant object of their thoughts.

In the Free States, on the contrary, from twenty to twenty-five millions of whites exist, with proportionate superiority in wealth, activity, and physical power, without any care of or danger from slaves.

This difference of condition in the two species of States produces unavoidably, in slaveholders, a continual sense of danger from within, and of prospective danger from without. The immense superiority of physical power in the Free States, combined with a knowledge of their own inherent weakness, creates in their minds a belief that their own political existence, and that of their slaves, depends upon obtaining and keeping the control of the Free States. Nature, in the human as in every other animal, compensates positive or comparative weakness by some quality which is equivalent for defence. In the case of the Slave States, she supplies the want of strength by *art*. The operation of this, in effecting their great object of obtaining and keeping the control of the Free States, it is my purpose briefly to illustrate from the history of this Union.

The *art* by which, for more than fifty years, the Slave States have subjugated the Free States, and vested in their own hands all the powers of the Union, they call *policy*. Its proper name is *cunning;* that "left-handed wisdom," as Lord Bacon calls it, which the Devil practised in the garden of Eden, — "divide and conquer." By this, they established the seat of national government in a slave country, and thus surrounded Congress with an atmosphere of slavery, and subjected the Free States to its influences, in the place where the councils of the nation are held, and where the whole public sentiment is hostile to the principles of the Free States; and where, in case of collisions resulting in actions at law and indictments, slaveholders are judges, jurors, and executioners. This location of the seat of government has been one of the most potent causes of that dominion over the nation which they have acquired.

Again: by *cunning*, they inserted Louisiana into the Union, not only without the concurrence of the Free States, but without so much as asking it, — a measure which has been the Pandora's box of all our evils.

Another of their arts is *arrogance*, or an insolent assumption of superiority. This, though a result of their condition as masters of slaves, is of great power. " Like boldness,* it is the child of ignorance and vanity; yet it fascinates, and binds, hand and foot, those that are shallow in judgment or weak in courage, and prevaileth even with wise men at weak times. It hath done wonders in popular States." In Slave States, slaveholders are sovereigns, and deem themselves entitled to govern everywhere. In them, with few inconsiderable exceptions, they are proprietors of all the lands; which few persons can afford to hold, except owners of slaves. As the rate of wages is regulated by the expense of supporting slaves, it is, of course, the least possible. Of consequence, slaves are the successful rivals of the *white poor;* being more obedient, and the expense of supporting them being less. Thus the *white poor*, in the Slave States, are reduced to a state of extreme degradation; in some respects, lower than the negro. They cannot dig; for field-labor to a white person is there a disgrace. To beg, they are ashamed; and they have no master to whom they can look for support. Having no land, they have no political power: the value of their labor is below that of the slave; and their actual condition comparatively that of extreme wretchedness. One-half

* Lord Bacon's Essay on Boldness.

of the white population of the Slave States are said to be in that condition.* In the vocabulary of slaveholders, liberty means only that planters should be independent, and have no superiors.

Educated under circumstances which make pride, and exercise of power, the chief elements of their character, they come to Congress with the arrogant spirit of aristocratic despots; looking down on the Representatives of the Free States as an inferior class; jealous, fearful, and hating all talents which they cannot command; courting, coaxing, fawning on all who will become their tools, so long as they are obedient, — when their servility is no longer useful, throwing them away with contempt. The different states of society expand this arrogance. It is well known, that, in the Free States, there is no honor in fighting a duel; that, in most of them, to give or accept a challenge would put an end to a man's hope of political advancement. It is also well known that the public sentiment is altogether the reverse in the Slave States. In these, to fight a duel is an evidence of gallantry. To kill a man in a duel is a glory, not a disgrace. Life itself depreciates, where killing a slave is often venial. For shooting a schoolmaster through the brain for whipping a refractory boy, juries acquit. According to the standard by which distributive justice is dispensed in a slaveholder's court in the city of Washington, three hundred dollars is an ample retribution

* Since this address was in the press, a citizen of Virginia has been compelled to leave the State, having had his life threatened for uttering the language of Washington in respect of slavery. His statements corroborate those contained in this address relative to the depressed state of the *laboring white men* in Slave States. There are now probably thousands of noble-spirited slaveholders in those States, who are true to the character, and partake of the spirit and virtues, of Washington, who dare not express their coincidence, through fear of the violence of those who at present possess the sovereignty in them. It will be a disgrace to the Free States, if they do not, at the ensuing election, come to their relief, and put out of power in the councils of the nation this degenerate class of slaveholders. — See the statements of Mr. Underwood, of Virginia, in the "New-York Herald," and other papers of the day.

for an assault, endangering life and future usefulness, made by a member of the House of Representatives upon a Senator sitting in his seat in the Senate Chamber of the United States!

This different state of sentiment and opinion, in the different sections of the United States, brings into action, in Congress, that arrogance, which, as has been stated, is an inseparable element of a slaveholder's character. The disposition to insult, and endeavor to browbeat, whoever from the Free States dares to cross his path, is excited into constant action, not only from the belief, that, towards members from the Free States, they can do it with impunity, but from the fact that such bullying is a sure path to popularity among their own constituents. Their boastful chivalric bravery is, in truth, only disguised cowardice. The slaveholder knows, that, if he does not display an alacrity to fight, he is disgraced at home, and can never hope to be sent to Congress afterwards; so that his vaunted courage is nothing but *fear* of being disgraced among his own constituents, and losing his political standing by showing what they call "the white feather."

To a man from the Free States, who gives or accepts a challenge, no term of reproach is too severe. By such act, he descends from the moral and religious elevation, on which the state of civilization in the Free States has placed him, to the semi-barbarous level of chivalric morality. For his fictitious courage, he is not supported in his trembling, as is the other, by fear of the corrupt opinion of his constituents. He fights with the knowledge that the act disgraces him at home; that, if he kills his antagonist, he is there ruined for life; that, if he is killed himself, he dieth as the fool dieth, — lying down, not in a bed of honor, but of disgrace. And deservedly; for he abandons the pure civilized code of true honor in which he has been educated, and heartlessly transfers his allegiance to a code of false honor, invented by barbarous chieftains in the middle ages to support their projects of plunder and tyranny, and naturally adopted in this more civilized age, by aristocratic dealers in slaves, to support the system by which they live, and which they hope to perpetuate by making it universal.*

Several years ago, John Quincy Adams said to me, "Insult, bullying, and threat characterize the slaveholders in Congress; talk, *timidity*, and submission, the Representatives from the Free States." What Adams calls "*timidity*," is in them, for the reasons above stated, for the most part unavoidable. Men educated under moral, religious, and refined influences, meet in Congress a class of men, of which, at home, they know nothing, and would not willingly meet anywhere; with many of whom, every second word is an oath; and who are always ready, with a pistol, or offer of a duel, to support what they call their arguments. This class was always in Congress. Formerly they were only a part of the slaveholders in the two branches; now they probably constitute a majority. These men are always ready to insult, threaten, and bully any member of Congress from the Free States who dares to retort their obloquy; which, if he does, a duel is thrust into his face, as was recently into Mr. Wilson's, and which he so honorably repelled, in the temper and demeanor of a mild, firm spirit of civilized chivalry. Although the natural tendency of slavery is to deteriorate the morals and weaken the self-control of the masters of slaves, yet there always have been men raised in the Slave States with an innate purity capable of repelling the influences of their condition, and endowed by nature with an herculean strength to strangle in man-

* These animadversions I have been compelled to make out of regard to truth and duty. No man can regret more than myself their apparent application to the course pursued by Mr. Burlingame, which, in every other respect, was wise, lofty, and honorable. His mistakes were, first, in admitting, by his act, that there could be, by any possibility, honor connected with duelling; and, second, in descending to the level of such an antagonist.

hood the serpents in whose coils their childhood and youth have been reared.

Fifty years ago, there were two classes of slaveholders in Congress; the one, generous in spirit, polished in manners, true to the principles of liberty and the Constitution, uniting heart and hand with the Representatives from the Free States in objects and policy; of the same type and character as George Washington, John Marshall, William Pinckney, Henry W. Dessaussure, John Stanley, Nicholas Vandyke, Philip Stuart, Alexander Contee Hanson, and a host of others, too numerous to be recapitulated, in principle and views coincident with the Constitution, destitute of all desire to establish the supremacy of slaveholders. They spoke of slavery, like Patrick Henry, as "a curse," which blighted the prospects and weakened the strength of the Slave States,—with him deplored the necessity of holding men in bondage, declaring their belief that the time would come when "an opportunity will be afforded *to abolish* this lamentable evil;" like Governor Randolph, they regarded themselves "oppressed by slavery, and treated with disdain the idea that the Slave States could stand by themselves;" * with Judge Tucker, of Virginia,† they thought, as he declared, that posterity "*would execrate the memory of those ancestors, who, having the power to avert the evil of slavery, have, like their first parents, entailed a curse on all future generations.*"

These men, far from threatening to go out of the Union, regarded and spoke of it as a main hope of dependence against their own slaves. They encouraged and supported every man from the Free States who met the violence of the insolent class with appropriate spirit. They saw and lamented the character and conduct of the lower and baser slaveholders, who, coarse in language, overbearing in man-

* See Debates in the Convention of Virginia.

† See Tucker's Commentaries on Blackstone.

ner, caring nothing for the principles of liberty and the Constitution, came to Congress for the purpose of getting office or place, and, to that end, were as subservient to every nod of the administration as any slave to that of his master.

The nobler class of slaveholders foresaw and foretold that the effect of the language and course of conduct of this violent class would gradually wear away the affections of the Free States, and lead to a dissolution of the Union. These higher spirits could not submit to use the arts and language to obtain power to which the baser sort condescended, and, of consequence, lost their influence in their respective districts; to which these political filibusters succeeded, and came to Washington, some to follow and some to direct the course of the administration, by whom they were rewarded according to their talents, their violence, or their subserviency.

In 1810, John Randolph, in whose mind Virginia included all the South, said to me, "Virginia is no longer what it once was. The spirit of the old planters is departed or gradually wearing away: we are overrun by time-servers office-hunters, and political blacklegs." In a letter to me, dated "Richmond, 22d March, 1814," after giving a melancholy description of a visit he had just made to "the seat of his ancestors, in the maternal line, at the confluence of the James and Appomattox Rivers," he adds, "*The curse of slavery, however, an evil daily magnifying, great as it already is, imbitters many a moment of the Virginian landholder, who is not duller than the clod under his feet.*" And, recurring to the then-existing state of Virginia, in the same letter he adds, "In your country, the state of society is not changed, the whole fabric uprooted, as it is with us. Here the rich vulgar are everybody and every thing. You can almost smell the rum and cheese and loaf and lump-sugar out of which their mushroom fortunes have sprung, much more offensive to my nostrils than 'muck and merinos.' These fellows will never 'get out of Black Friars;' and they make up in ostentation for other deficiencies of which they are always conscious, and sometimes ashamed."

Slaveholders have been for fifty years, a few only excepted, the political masters of these States. Rampant with long-possessed authority, in the natural spirit of the class, they have now put on the lash, and are getting ready for use their fetters and manacles.

Let the Free States understand that the crisis has come. Their own fate and that of their posterity depend upon the fact, whether, in this crisis, they are true or false to themselves. The extension of slavery has been, from the days of Jefferson, the undeviating pursuit of the slaveholders. Hitherto by cunning, intrigue, and corruption, and now to plant it for ever among the South-western States, compromises have been violated, the ballot-boxes broken, the votes of freemen destroyed, and free citizens massacred and their houses plundered by mobs, encouraged by a slaveholder's administration, and supported by the military arm of the United States. If this tissue of events do not rouse the Free States to united and concentrated action, nothing will. Their destinies are fixed. They are doomed slaves. Their liberties are gone, their Constitution gone. Nothing is left to them but to yoke in with the negro, and take the lash, submissively, at the caprice of their masters.

But everybody asks, "What is to be done to throw off this slaveholders' yoke?" The first step is to have a spirit and will to be free. If there is a will, the spirit of freemen will soon find a way. It is not the slaveholders' strength, but your folly. It is because they wake, and you sleep; because they unite, and you divide; because they hold in their hands the means of corruption, and half of you perhaps are willing to be corrupted. This is bold language, it will be said. Boldness is one of the privileges of old age. When can a man have a right to be bold, if it be not when he is conscious of being prompted by truth and duty alone, and when a long life is behind him, and nothing before him but a daily-expected summons to the highest and most solemn of all tribunals?

I now proceed to trace the political power of these slaveholders from its origin, and show the present actual condition of the Constitution, *as it is called*, of the United States.

It has been already stated that the *cunning* of the slaveholders was early developed in two measures, — the establishment of the seat of government in a slave country, and the admission of Louisiana into the Union without the assent of the people of the United States. To the effects of the first, I have already alluded. Those of the second were known and acknowledged by the leaders of the councils of the nation, at the time of its adoption, to be a *gross violation of the Constitution of the United States;* that it was a power the people of the States never granted to Congress. That such was the fact, no man at this day does or can deny, except those who, for party purposes or personal ends, are ready to say or do any thing.

The admission of Louisiana into the Union, without asking or having the consent of the people of the States or of the States themselves, was undeniably a *stupendous usurpation.*

Now, there is no advice more distinctly given, no warning more solemnly uttered, by Washington, in that "Farewell Address to the People of the United States" which is called his legacy, than this, — "LET THERE BE NO CHANGE BY USURPATION." That the admission of Louisiana into the Union, without the assent of the Free States, was *a gross violation of the Constitution, and a stupendous usurpation* of powers not given them by the Constitution, there can be no possible question. That it was such, was known and declared by Thomas Jefferson himself, then President of the United States. In a letter to a Mr. Breckenridge, dated

August the 12th, 1803, stating the course to be pursued for the admission of Louisiana, he unreservedly writes: "*Congress must appeal to the nation for an additional article to the Constitution*, approving and confirming an act which they must previously pass for its admission. . . . *The Constitution has made no provision for our holding foreign territory, still less for incorporating foreign nations into our Union.*" * And in a letter to Wilson Cary Nicholas, dated "Monticello, Sept. 7, 1803," Mr. Jefferson enters into a laborious argument to show that "it was not the intention of the Constitution to permit Congress to admit into the Union new States in Territories not included within the limits of the old United States;" intimates that doing so "*would make the Constitution blank paper by construction;* adding, that, "if the powers granted are considered '*boundless,*' *then we have no Constitution;*" and concludes by declaring it "*important, in the present case, to set an example against broad construction, by appealing to the people for new powers.*" †

It will throw light on the path of the duty of the Free

* See Jefferson's Works, vol. iii. p. 512.

† The language of Mr. Jefferson is as follows: "I am aware of the force of the observations you make on the power given by the Constitution to Congress to admit new States into the Union, without restraining the subject to the territory then constituting the United States. But when I consider that the limits of the United States are precisely fixed by the treaty of 1783, that the Constitution expressly declares itself to be made for the United States, I cannot help believing the intention was not to permit Congress to admit into the Union new States which should be formed out of the territory for which, and under whose authority alone, they were then acting. I do not believe it was meant that they might receive England, Ireland, Holland, &c., into it; which would be the case, on your construction. When an instrument admits two constructions, — the one safe, the other dangerous; the one precise, the other indefinite, — I prefer that which is safe and precise. I had rather ask an enlargement of power from the nation, where it is found necessary, than to assume it by a construction which would make our powers boundless. Our peculiar security is in the possession of a written Constitution. *Let us not make it a blank paper by construction.* I say the same as to the opinion of those who consider the grant of the treaty-making power as boundless. *If it is, then we have no Constitution.*"

"I confess, then, I think it important, in the present case, to set an example against broad construction, by appealing for new power to the people." — *Jefferson's Letter to Wilson Cary Nicholas, dated Monticello, Sept.* 7, 1803. *See Jefferson's Writings, edition* 1830, vol. iv. pp. 2, 3.

States to show how this *stupendous usurpation* was first effected, and for them to learn the workings of that *cunning*, which, as has been stated, is a main element of the power of slaveholders.

When the leading slaveholders in Congress found that their great head, President Jefferson, had taken ground on *a strict construction of the Constitution*, they at once perceived, that, if his principles were adopted, there would be an end of their great project of enlarging the sphere of slavery by admitting into the Union territories beyond the old limits of the United States. They saw at once, that, if the question of admission should be referred to the people or the States for decision, the consequences would be foreseen by them; it would be negatived, or the admission clogged with such conditions or limitations as would not only defeat, in this case, the great project of the slaveholders, but, what was worse, preclude the enlargement of their power, by inserting new Slave States in territories, obtained by acquisition or conquest, lying beyond Louisiana itself. For the precedent once established, that Congress had no power in such cases, but that application to the people of the States must first be made, the slaveholders would be defeated in their project for ever. Under these apprehensions, they set themselves at work to satisfy Mr. Jefferson that the clause in the Constitution relative to the admission of new States was, without restriction, to the territory of the United States. Thus these slaveholders, who at every period of our history, before and since, have made *strict construction* their clamor and their policy, now saw nothing exceptionable in advocating the broadest of all possible constructions, because they saw, in its consequences, enlargement of the slaveholders' power. Jefferson declared that he was not convinced by their arguments, but "*that he was willing to let the bill pass*," intimating that he would not interpose his *veto;* although, at the same time, he avowed it "*would make* *the Constitution a blank paper by construction*." Seeing the great benefit which would result to the slaveholders' power, "*whatever Congress should think it necessary to do*," he was ready to sanction. "*If our friends should think differently from me, I shall acquiesce with satisfaction*."* He did not pretend that his conscience was convinced, or his sense of duty altered; but, seeing the benefit which would redound to the slaveholders, he would not obstruct the passage of the bill.

The course he recommended his partisans to pursue, in order to conceal his opinion from the people of the Free States, and keep them deceived and ignorant of the consequences of the act, — which, in opposition to his declared opinion that it would make a nullity of the Constitution, he consented to let pass, — is characteristic of the slaveholders' *cunning*. Finding that, by influence, by hopes of place, or by office, they could command votes enough from the Free States to effect their purposes, Jefferson thus confidentially develops his policy. In a letter to Levi Lincoln, dated "Monticello, Aug. 30, 1803," he thus wrote: "*Concerning the admission of Louisiana*, THE LESS THAT IS SAID ABOUT ANY CONSTITUTIONAL DIFFICULTY THE BETTER."† And in his letter to Wilson Cary Nicholas, above cited, writing on the same subject, he says, "*Whatever Congress shall think it necessary to do* SHOULD BE DONE WITH AS LITTLE DEBATE AS POSSIBLE, PARTICULARLY AS FAR AS RESPECTS THE CONSTITUTIONAL DIFFICULTY." Here we see developed the arts of the slaveholder, and the source of that insolence and browbeating by which in that day every man was assailed who exposed the nature of the bill for admitting Louisiana, and dared to state the consequences, resulting from its passage, in the very words and on the

* See Jefferson's Letter to Wilson Cary Nicholas, dated Monticello, Sept. 7, 1803.

† Jefferson's Writings, vol. iv. p. 1.

very principles which his partisans knew were held and maintained by Jefferson himself.

The passage of the Louisiana Admission Bill was effected by the arts which slaveholders well know how to select and apply. Sops were given to the congressional watch-dogs of the Free States. To some, promises were made, by way of opiates; and those whom they could neither pay nor drug were publicly treated with insolence and scorn. Threats, duels, and violence were at that day, as now, modes approved by them to deter men from awakening the Free States to a sense of their danger. From the moment that act was passed, they saw that the Free States were shorn of their strength; that they had obtained space to multiply Slave States at their will; and Mr. Jefferson had confidentially told them, that, from that moment, the "*Constitution of the United States was blank paper;*" but more correctly, there was "*no longer any Constitution.*"

The slaveholders from that day saw they had the Free States in their power; that they were masters, and the Free States slaves; and have acted accordingly. From the passage of the Louisiana Bill until this day, their policy has been directed to a single object, with almost uninterrupted success. That object was to exclude the Free States from any share of power, except in subserviency to their views; and they have undeniably, during all the subsequent period of our history (the administration of John Quincy Adams only excepted), placed in the chair of state either slaveholders, or men from the Free States, who, for sake of power, consented to be their tools, — "Northern men with Southern principles;" in other words, men who, for the sake of power or pay, were willing to do any work they would set them upon.

In the times of non-intercourse and embargo, I had frequent intercourse with John Randolph, and for many years a correspondence with him. During the extreme pressure of those measures upon the commerce of the Northern States, I said to him, " Mr. Randolph, these measures are absolutely insupportable. You Southern men will, at this rate, put an end to parties in the Northern States, and we shall come down upon the South in one united phalanx." I shall never forget the half-triumph and half-sneer with which he replied, "*You are mistaken, sir; you are mistaken, sir.* THE SOUTH ARE AS SURE OF YOUR DEMOCRACY AS THEY ARE OF THEIR OWN NEGROES."

Let any man examine the history of the United States, from the reign of Thomas Jefferson to that of Franklin Pierce, and he will find, that, when the slaveholders have any particularly odious and obnoxious work to do, they never fail to employ the leaders of the democracy of the Free States. This fact speaks volumes to the Free States. In all estimates of their future duties, it should never be forgotten, that every act by which their interests have been sacrificed, and the power of slaveholders increased, has been effected by the treachery of members of the Free States.

That the people of the Free States might, on the admission of Louisiana into the Union without their consent, have declared the Constitution so violated as to justify them in dissolving the Union, no one, who takes the authority and principles of Jefferson as his guide, can doubt. If the people of the Free States had then foreseen one-tenth of the consequences which they realize at this day, can it be questioned but they would have liberated themselves from that prospective thraldom to which they, in consequence, are now subjected? Could they have foreseen that the effect of that bill would have been to invest the comparatively insignificant body of slaveholders with the power of multiplying Slave States at their will in these new-acquired territories, and also into others, admitted by virtue of this precedent; that by these means that infamous and doubly deceptive principle, whereby *property*, under the mask of *persons*, is admitted to a representation, nominally of persons in bondage, in fact a representation of their masters, the oppressor representing the oppressed; — could it have been, in that day, possibly anticipated that the result of that admission would have been to multiply and extend the power of that false and iniquitous principle to an indefinite degree, not only into the territories then acquired, but into other lands, invaded and conquered for no other reason than enlarging the sphere of that abominable principle, in consequences of which all the proportions of representation between the Slave and Free States, established by the Constitution, have been annihilated; — can it be questioned, that the Free States would have at once cut adrift from these slaveholders, or, more wisely, have intimated a sense of their comparative insignificance, by rejecting the Louisiana Bill, or demanding admission of that State upon such terms as would have secured for ever to the Free States that proportion of power which the original provision of the Constitution had guaranteed to them?

While the Louisiana Bill was in its passage, it was said openly, by the author of this address, in Congress, "*If this bill passes, the bonds of this Union are virtually dissolved; the States which compose it are free from their moral obligations; and that as it will be the right of all, so it will be the duty of some, to prepare definitely for a separation, — peaceably if they can, violently if they must.*" The results and duties then stated are as true and incumbent at the present as they were at that day. The only difference is, that what was then but foreseen is now realized; what was then prophecy is now history.

It is, then, manifest to the Free States, that a *monstrous usurpation has been effected*, and is intended to be enlarged and perpetuated.

The warning voice of Washington, in this state of things, is, "LET THERE BE NO CHANGE BY USURPATION." He adds, "CHANGE BY USURPATION IS THE CUSTOMARY WEAPON BY WHICH FREE GOVERNMENTS ARE DESTROYED." Again: Washington advises, "RESIST WITH CARE THE SPIRIT OF INNOVATION UPON THE PRINCIPLES OF THE CONSTITUTION. THE SPIRIT OF ENCROACHMENT TENDS TO CONSOLIDATE THE POWERS OF ALL DEPARTMENTS IN ONE, AND THUS TO CREATE A REAL DESPOTISM."

Let the inhabitants of the Free States look into history, and see whether the spirit of encroachment has not already consolidated in the hands of slaveholders *the powers of all the departments.* Is there an officer of State, from the President downwards, who has not been selected from the knowledge or belief of his adhesion to the slaveholders' supremacy? The tenants of all the offices, which give to their possessors daily bread, are of course holden to servitude to the slaveholders by the necessities of existence. Inquire, and see, whether, since the days of Andrew Jackson, the selections of the judges of your courts of judicature, even of the highest, have not been made in consequence of hard political services rendered, or from principles previously avowed of the nature of a declaration of subserviency to the slaveholders' power.

The Free States are then, undeniably, at this day, in that very state of things in which the warning voice of Washington declared "RESISTANCE TO BE THEIR DUTY." During more than forty years, the spirit of a continued series of encroachments has established over them *the worst of all possible despotisms,* — THAT OF SLAVEHOLDERS. The manner in which this duty of resistance, so distinctly advised by Washington, is to be performed in the spirit which he advised, and which his life exemplified, is at this time the subject of earnest and solicitous consideration by the people of the Free States. It will be my endeavor to throw some light on their duties, and on the course to be pursued in performing them.

The duties of the Free States result, first, from their political condition. Of this, in respect of the Constitution of 1789, there can be no doubt. In 1811, members from the Free States declared in Congress that the passage of the bill admitting Louisiana rendered the Constitution of the United States *a blank letter;* or, rather, that thereafter there was no Constitution. In that day, Thomas Jefferson, the great leader of the so-called "Democratic Republicans," declared the same thing.

The continuance in union at that time was simply a question of *expediency*, and has so continued until the present. To the Free States, their continuance in this connection has ever since been, and is now, not the result of moral obligation, but solely of *expediency.* This condition of things is the first element from which the Free States are bound to deduce their duties.

The next is the character of the people of the Slave States, and the utter incompatibility of that character with the liberties of the Free States, *so long as the controlling powers of government are permitted to remain in the hands of slaveholders.* The character of slaveholders results from their ownership of slaves. The very basis of their political condition is not liberty, but slavery. The equality which liberty establishes among freemen and Free States they neither appreciate nor can understand. With them, equality means, and can mean, only equality among masters of slaves. To live by the labor of fellow-beings is their notion of happiness. To live idly and luxuriously themselves, to govern others, and appropriate to their own use the fruits of other persons' industry, is the substance of their felicity. Never to do any thing for themselves which they can make others do for them, is the principle of their actions. *Labor* is with them only another name for *servi-*

*tude.* Those who labor are held in the same contempt, and thought entitled to the same treatment, as are their own negroes. Many years ago, John Quincy Adams related a conversation which he once had with John C. Calhoun on this very subject. Calhoun said to him, that the broad principles of liberty which Mr. Adams had been advocating were just and noble; but that in the Southern country, whenever they were mentioned, they were always understood as applying only to *white men.* Domestic labor was confined to the blacks; and such was the prejudice, that if he, who was the most popular man in his district, were to keep a white servant in his house, his character and reputation would be irretrievably ruined. Mr. Adams said, that this confounding servitude and labor was one of the bad effects of slavery. Mr. Calhoun thought it was attended with many excellent consequences. It did not apply to all sorts of labor, — not, for example, to holding the plough; he and his father had often done that: nor did it apply to manufacturing and mechanical labor; these were not degrading: but to dig, to hoe, to do work either in the field, the house, or the stable, — these were menial labors, the proper work of slaves. No white man could descend to that. Calhoun thought that it was the best guarantee of equality among the whites. It produced among them an unvarying level. It did not admit of inequalities among whites. Mr. Adams replied, that it was all perverted sentiment, mistaking labor for slavery, and dominion for freedom. And, in stating it in conversation, Adams remarked, that this discussion with Calhoun had betrayed to him the secret of their souls. In the abstract, they admit slavery to be an evil; but, when probed to the quick, they show, at the bottom of their souls, pride and vainglory in their very condition of masterdom. They fancy themselves more generous and noble-hearted than the plain freemen that labor for subsistence. They look down on the simplicity of New-England manners, because they have no habits of overbearing like theirs, and cannot treat negroes like dogs. It is among the evils of slavery, that it taints the very sources of moral principle. It establishes false estimates of virtue and vice; for what can be more false and heartless than this doctrine, which makes the first and holiest rights of humanity depend on the color of the skin? It perverts human reason, and reduces man, endowed with logical powers, to maintain that slavery is sanctioned by the Christian religion; that slaves are happy and contented in their condition; that there are, between master and slave, mutual ties of attachment and affection; that the virtues of the master are refined and exalted by the degradation of the slave; while, at the same time, they vent execrations on the slave-trade, curse Great Britain for having given them slaves, burn at the stake negroes convicted of crimes, for the terror of the example, and writhe in agonies of fear at the very mention of human rights as applicable to people of color. "The impression produced on my mind," Mr. Adams added, "by this discussion, is, that the bargain between freedom and slavery, contained in the Constitution of the United States, is morally and politically vicious, inconsistent with the principles on which alone our revolution can be justified, cruel and oppressive by riveting the chains of slavery, by pledging the faith of freedom to maintain and perpetuate the tyranny of the master, and grossly unequal and impolitic by admitting that slaves are at once enemies to be kept in subjection, property to be secured and returned to their owners, and persons not to be represented themselves, but for whom their masters are privileged with nearly a double share of representation. The consequence has been, that this slave representation has governed the Union. Benjamin's portion above his brethren has ravined as a wolf. In the morning he has devoured the prey, and in the evening has divided the spoil.

It would be no difficult matter to prove, by recurring to the history of the Union under this Constitution, that almost every thing which has contributed to the honor and welfare of this nation has been accomplished in despite of them, or forced upon them; and every thing unpropitious and dishonorable may be traced to them."

After reading and weighing the opinions of this great and good man, and reflecting on the facts which he states, can any one doubt the incompatibility of the essential character of slaveholders with the government and management of the affairs of freemen? Can they who regard labor as servitude be the fit guardians of the interests of men who regard labor as their honor, and its successful exercise their duty and glory?

Mr. Jefferson, in his "Notes on Virginia," graphically exhibits "the unhappy influence on the manners of slaveholders by the existence of slavery. The whole commerce between master and slave is a perpetual exercise of the most boisterous passions; the most unremitting despotism on the one part, and degrading submission on the other. Our children see this, learn to imitate it; for man is an imitative animal. This quality is the germ of all education in him. From his cradle to his grave, he is learning to do what he sees others do. If a parent could find no motive, either in his philanthropy or self-love, for restraining the intemperance of passion towards his slave, it should always be a sufficient one that his child is present; but, in general, it is not sufficient. The parent storms; the child looks on, catches the lineaments of wrath, puts on the same airs in the circle of smaller slaves, gives a loose to his worst passions, and, thus nursed, educated, and daily exercised in tyranny, cannot but be stamped with odious peculiarities. The man, then, must be a prodigy who can retain his morals and manners undepraved by such circumstances."

After such testimony, given by the greatest and most

idolized of all slaveholders, as to the qualities which are the necessary results of their education from childhood of his whole class, will the people of the Free States trust them longer with the care of their Union? Is it wonderful, that in every year, from the days of Thomas Jefferson to the present, such men as Brooks, Keitt, and Butler should, in one uninterrupted succession, have appeared on the floor of Congress?

Without enumerating other qualities inherent in slaveholders, and incompatible with the liberties of the Free States, I proceed to examine the nature of that power which slaveholders have wielded over this Union for half a century.

How is it that a body of slaveholders, which at no previous period have exceeded in numbers more than three hundred thousand, and which at this day do not equal three hundred and fifty thousand, — of which certainly not more than one thousand have any weight or voice in devising and conducting their policy, — have been able, for more than fifty years, to lead from eighteen to twenty millions of men whithersoever they will, and to establish over them a sovereignty which is yet to be proved not immovable and permanent?

This power of slaveholders has its origin, — as has been already intimated, — first, from a concentration of interests and fears in the body of slaveholders; second, from a total want of concentration of interests among the people of the Free States, combined with an entire want of all apprehensions of danger, owing to their unquestionable superiority in physical power. This, then, is the exact state of things in this Union. There are in it about three hundred thousand slaveholders, whose interests and fears are identical. There are in it at least from twenty to twenty-four millions of men in the Free States, who have no special identity of interest, and absolutely no fear whatsoever. This state of things is one of the sources from which the power slaveholders wield emanates. Their slaves are at once their pride and their weakness, the objects of their dependence and their fears. In 1811, John Randolph, who, with all his eccentricities, was the truest to his class and the most honorable of all slaveholders, and who saw with contempt the blustering bravadoes of many of his brethren, thus exposed their weakness and their terrors on the floor of Congress: "While you are talking of taking Canada, some of us are shuddering for our own safety at home. I speak from facts, when I say that the night-bell never tolls for fire, in Richmond, that the mother does not hug her infant more closely to her bosom. I have been witness of some alarms in the capital of Virginia." *

How greatly the terror of their slave population has increased since the days of John Randolph, may be conceived from the following facts. Then the slave population but little exceeded *one million;* now it greatly exceeds *three millions.*

From the identity of the interests and fears of slaveholders results identity in policy of the members of the whole class. Their studies, thoughts, counsels, are absorbed and directed to two objects, — how to keep their negroes in subjection; and, as subsidiary to this end, how to keep the control of the Free States. By this control, they present to the fears of their slaves the arm of the Union, ever in readiness to keep them in subjection, and also relieve themselves from the apprehension that that arm might be extended for the relief of their slaves.

The different state of society in the Slave and Free States, of itself, gives the former advantages over the latter, for obtaining control of the affairs of the Union. It is well known that the Free States cannot, from their state of

* See Life of John Randolph by Hugh S. Garland, vol. i. p. 294.

society, always send their best men to Congress. They are often compelled, from the circumstances in which Heaven has placed them, to labor, in their respective vocations, for the support of themselves and their families. They have no negroes to make work for them when they are away, none that they can sell to make up the deficiencies of their income while they are absent. The Slave States, on the contrary, can always command their best men, — best not from morals, not from virtues, nor yet from talents, but best for their purposes. The slaveholders form a class of slaveholding aristocratic landholders, who take up the trade of democracy in order to get possession of and victimize the leaders of the democracies of the Free States. They know that these leaders have generally not one spice of democracy in their composition, but, like themselves, have taken up that trade for the sake of power, and who naturally fall into the slaveholders' arms from likeness of object and instinctive sympathy. They have not, like the slaveholder, any negroes of their own, but are ready, as John Randolph would say, at any moment, to become negro to the slaveholder, provided they can get place or pay, or the fodder they desire. These men never trouble themselves what services the slaveholders will require. They are ready to vote for them in order to make new Slave States in the old-acquired territories; or to fight for them in order to conquer new territories in which to extend the area of slavery; or to assist them in breaking down the barrier, erected by compromise, to prevent its farther extension; and, to maintain the slaveholders' triumph, do not hesitate to dip their hands in the blood of their brethren of the Free States.

The slaveholders' mode of operation in extending their power is well worthy analysis. Having no necessity nor inclination to labor, those of them who have, from their great wealth, more idle time than the generality, devote themselves to politics; which, in their vocabulary, means how to govern their slaves and how to control the Free States. Those being kept in subjection through fear of the arm of the Union, the main study of the slaveholder is how to keep this arm in subjection to them. This is the topic of discussion at their homes, in their court-houses, their caucuses, and in their senate-chambers. In their plantations, they live in a species of lordly solitude. Though thus, mostly, they think and reason and write apart, yet, from the identity of their interests and fears, their thoughts and reasonings result in the same line of policy, which, at their general meetings, they agree upon and settle. Though widely separate, the chiefs sit as spiders in the centre of their respective webs, throwing out filaments to every State in the Union, in every one of which the threads of some of them find points of attachment and reciprocation, in custom-houses, post-offices, those of contracting printers, and many others, from each of which ready sympathetic responses are returned, as sure and as quick as by the wires of the telegraph. These responses are collected at Washington, in which the character and qualification of each member of Congress is as well known as at his own home.

How to secure and manage those members of Congress who are likely to take a lead in debate, or exert any influence in either branch, never fails to be a special study of the slaveholders, which is greatly facilitated by the location of Congress in the city of Washington. Such men from the Free States soon become objects of attention of men well versed in the arts of governing slaves, and of winning white men to their purposes; and while the new member is, perhaps, wondering what makes him such a special object of kindness, and is thinking only how to reciprocate, they are examining him as an article in the market, — whether he can be bought at all; whether he is worth buying; whether, if bought, he has sufficient influence at home to carry his whole district with him. These questions settled to the satisfaction of the slaveholders, and the certainty established that there will be no flinching, however hard the service they may exact, the price at which he can be had being ascertained, will in due time be paid, whether it be by a place in the customs, or in the post-office, or in the cabinet, or an embassy in Europe or in China, and mayhap, if he stand trial in the hardest service, by even the President's chair.

Let the people look into the history of the Union ever since the days of Andrew Jackson, and they can trace the services to the slaveholders, by which men from the Free States have attained their offices, and see the humbleness of the servility with which they have executed all the orders of the slaveholders. Such research into history will show the remarkable tact with which they seek and select among the leaders of the democracies of the great States, always securing for their service the most corrupt and the least scrupulous; and what atrocious services they have performed for their masters, history also tells.

I recur to these facts, and to history in support of them, not because there is any thing new in them, they having been at every period subjects of common and general observation, but by way of warning to the Free States, from the voice of history, of what they may always expect, so long as they permit slaveholders to manage the affairs of the Union; and to urge upon them the duty, if they mean to be either safe or free, to unite as one man, and to take the affairs of the Union into their own hands, and allow slaveholders no other proportion of influence or power than they were invested with by the Constitution of the United States, when it came from the hands of George Washington.

I have thus endeavored to illustrate the arts and operations by which slaveholders have acquired and held, with but few exceptions, the control of this Union for more than fifty years. In every stage of their successful power, they have had the aid of men who neither themselves nor their constituents were slaveholders.

The history of our Union is little else than a record of the triumphs of slavery, through the instrumentality of the ambition, cupidity, and baseness of men from the Free States. They aided the slaveholders in the calumnies and falsehoods by which Washington and his friends were first thrust out of power. When Jefferson, contrary to his avowed convictions, consented to make the Constitution of the United States a dead letter, for the purpose of opening an indefinitely wide field for the extension of the slave power, men from the Free States seconded his plans, and assisted in their execution. Without one trace of democracy in their hearts, more than Louis Napoleon has in his, men from the Free States took up democracy as a trade, thus obtained influence in the Free States, connected themselves with every administration which would accept their services, content even "to be sutlers to the camp since profits would accrue." Through the influence of such men, who have been successively little else than traitors to the great interest of the Free States, to liberty, humanity, and the progress of civilization, the slaveholder has taken possession of every arm of the Union, even of the fountains of justice itself.

The fact, therefore, is not extraordinary, that a taint of slave influence can be seen and shown in the morals, literature, and religion of the Free States, — in their halls of justice and halls of liberty. If life, health, and mind be preserved to me, what is here but a suggestion shall be made manifest in detail.

The Free States have been so long terrified or fascinated by the serpent Slavery, that escape from its folds seemed hopeless, until a kind Providence, watching over the destinies of this nation, has at length permitted it to exhibit itself in its true character, — violent, lawless, unprincipled, insolent, and overbearing; prostrating liberty in the senate-chamber at Washington, its jaws red with the blood of free citizens at Kansas.

More than fifty years' attentive observation of the operations of the slave power in this Union compels me to declare, that the provision of the Constitution of the United States which gave to them the weight of their slaves in the balance of power has been the *great misfortune* of this Union, and will be its destruction unless the Free States rally to its rescue, and take possession of the government. A longer continuance of it in the hands of slaveholders seems practically impossible.

I know, that, on this subject, the Free States are always ominously told, "that, if the Slave States cannot continue to govern the Union, *they will go out of it.*" It is a question of some curiosity, where, in such case, these emigrating gentlemen will go, and what they will do with that living, slippery luggage they must carry with them.

In 1820, when the Missouri-Compromise question was in debate, John Calhoun said to John Quincy Adams, "that he did not believe that the question then pending in Congress would produce a dissolution of the Union; but, if it should, *the South would be, from necessity, compelled to form an alliance, offensive and defensive, with Great Britain.*" Mr. Adams asked "if that would not be returning to the Colonial state." Calhoun said, "Yes, pretty much; but it would be forced upon them." Mr. Adams inquired "whether he thought, if, by the effect of this alliance, offensive and defensive, the population of the North should be cut off from its natural outlet upon the ocean, it would fall back upon its rocks, bound hand and foot, to starve, or whether it would not retain its powers of locomotion to move southward by land." Mr. Calhoun replied, "Then it would be necessary for the South *to make their communities all military.*" Thus this glorious plan of "going out of the Union" will result, according to Mr. Calhoun's opinion, first in a return to a state of Colonial subjection to Great Britain; and, second, to a hopeful independence under the military prowess of *three hundred thousand whites* to keep in subjection *three million of slaves.*

At the coming election, I cannot doubt that the Free States, in which the greatest proportion of practical wisdom, active talent, and efficient virtue exists, will take possession of this government; restore to the Constitution the proportions of power established by Washington; re-instate, in full force, that barrier against the extension of slavery, called "the Missouri Compromise;" make Kansas a Free State; and put an end for ever to the addition of any more Slave States to this Union, — duties to be fulfilled *at every hazard*, even of the dissolution of the Union itself. If this Union is destined to break to pieces, it cannot fall in a more glorious struggle than in the endeavor to limit the farther extension of slavery, — that disgrace of our nation, and curse of our race.

From the depths of the human heart, Nature, abjuring as she does all right of one man to have property in another, calls on the people of the Free States to be faithful to these duties. The spirit of Liberty, to whom Washington intrusted the preservation of this Union, calls on them to relieve her from the shame of being longer an instrument to propagate slavery, and a pander for oppression. Unborn millions, destined hereafter to fill the earth from the Mississippi to the Pacific, cry to them, from the depths of all future ages, to be faithful to their great trust; exclaiming, *"On your faithfulness it depends, whether we shall become the depraved subjects or ministers of a slave despotism; whether fraud, violence, and an infamous traffic, shall be our destiny, or the enjoyment of the pure light of liberty, morality, and religion."*

www.ingramcontent.com/pod-product-compliance
Lightning Source LLC
LaVergne TN
LVHW020741120826
845150LV00010B/2286

* 9 7 8 1 4 1 8 1 9 3 8 6 7 *